This journal belongs to:

How Am I Feeling Right Now?

How Am I Feeling Right Now?

A Mindfulness Journal
for Exploring My Emotions

SPRUCE BOOKS
A Sasquatch Books Imprint

Contents

Why It Is Important to Be Able to Describe Your Feelings

Being able to recognize and name your feelings is an essential skill for learning how to practice mindfulness.

There is a lot of talk about mindfulness as an important aspect of mental health these days, but what exactly is it? *Mindfulness* is the ability to notice what you are feeling in any given moment and to be aware of your feelings without judging, changing, or suppressing them.

The first part, *noticing what you are feeling in the moment*, is trickier than it may seem, because many of us have difficulty identifying what we are feeling. One reason for this is that it's not always easy to find the right words. When asked "How are you feeling right now?" we may struggle for something to say—indeed, our main feeling might be that we are literally at a loss for words. In that case, we may resort to a vague response like "I'm fine" or "Everything's OK." Sometimes we feel overwhelmed by the complexity of our feelings, and instead of trying to say what we are feeling, we go with an easier option and describe what we are doing, such as "Oh, I'm super busy." Other times we might avoid trying to sort through all the emotions and choose instead to report on our physical state: for example, "I'm sleepy."

It is easier to tap into what we are feeling and express it if we have the words available—our own vocabulary of feelings. Words, after all, are essential tools for recognizing and describing what we feel.

The second part, *being aware of your feelings without judging, changing, or suppressing them*, is also challenging for most people. Not all feelings are easy to deal with; sometimes they are confusing, surprising, distressing, intense, or otherwise difficult. Learning to accurately describe those feelings is the first step toward being able to just coexist with them. Fortunately, it gets easier the more you do it.

This guided journal is designed to help you with both aspects of mindfulness. It has two main features—starting on page 12, a list of hundreds of words to help you describe your feelings, and starting on page 21, a set of guided prompts to help you examine, explore, get used to, understand, and accept those feelings.

Why Practice Mindfulness?

There are many studies showing that individuals who practice mindfulness—who are able to notice and describe what they are feeling—tend to experience higher levels of health and happiness. They suffer less from depression and anxiety, have more satisfying relationships, are more resilient when faced with life's inevitable challenges, and are better able to recognize and respond appropriately to what other people are feeling. (See page 174 for further reading on this topic.)

These are some of the reasons why many evidence-based therapeutic approaches—including cognitive behavioral therapy (CBT), dialectical behavior therapy (DBT), and acceptance and commitment therapy (ACT)—incorporate mindfulness as part of their approach to improving mental and emotional health.

Mindfulness helps people learn to process their feelings in healthy ways. Feelings can be powerful, and if we do not know how to deal with them, we may try instead to ignore or smother them. Alternatively, we may overthink or obsess over them. When we can process our feelings in healthy ways, we are better able to handle life's challenges, large and small.

What's the Deal with All These Feelings?

Feelings are just information. When a feeling is intense, it's easy to believe that it represents a profound truth about yourself, the world, or your situation. But let's look a little closer at how feelings work.

Feelings are physical and mental. We feel things in our bodies and through our minds. Science is still charting the complicated ways in which mind and body interact. For the purposes of this journal, we will describe what we experience in our bodies as *sensations* and what we experience in our consciousness as *feelings*.

Feelings come and go. People experience a lot of feelings. Think about a typical day and how many different feelings you may have gone through. Some probably went by so quickly that you barely noticed, while others may have lingered longer—but none of them lasted forever. Feelings pass.

Feelings vary in intensity. They may be mild, overwhelming, or anything in between. The level of intensity tells us something about ourselves, but it is not an indication that the feeling is "true." And even the most intense feelings that you think will never change? They eventually pass too.

Feelings are neither good nor bad. Feelings are just feelings. They are not indicators that we are good or bad people, and they are not actions. Sometimes, however, it can be hard to accept what we are feeling, especially if the feeling is intense or uncomfortable. Sometimes our feelings can be scary. You might think "I shouldn't feel this way" or "I hate this feeling!" Reminding ourselves that feelings are just information can help us to accept them, rather than to judge them or condemn ourselves for having them.

We cannot control our feelings. Some feelings may make us uncomfortable, while others may fill us with delight. Attempting to control them—to hold onto feelings that we enjoy, or to reject or avoid feelings that make us uncomfortable—does not work. Trying to avoid or suppress a feeling can backfire, making it more intense or causing it to manifest in some other way, such as a physical symptom. Being able to accept that you have an uncomfortable feeling—and knowing that it will pass—gives you a powerful tool for handling those situations.

Putting feelings into words helps us deal with them. There is a lot of solid research that demonstrates how putting your feelings into words relieves stress and increases calmness. Scientists believe this is because when we activate the parts of our brains that are responsible for finding words, we lessen activity in the areas responsible for intense emotions. This gives us a pause during which we can reflect on the feelings and process them.

The way we express or act upon our feelings is up to us. While we cannot force ourselves to feel one way or another, we can choose the way we respond to our feelings. Expressing and understanding our feelings helps us to figure out how to *respond* rather than *react* to them—to thoughtfully choose positive, healthy actions instead of acting in the heat of the moment, which frequently leads to poor outcomes.

How to Use This Journal

This guided journal is divided into two main sections—the **Feelings List** and **Journaling Prompts**. The Feelings List is just what it sounds like: a collection of hundreds of words to describe the many sensations and feelings we can experience. While it doesn't claim to be totally comprehensive—we could not include every single feeling in the vast universe of human emotion—it should give you enough words that you can begin to accurately describe your feelings. There is also space for you to add feelings and sensations that are not listed.

The Journaling Prompts section is designed to help you connect with, explore, and accept your feelings without judgment. Answering the prompts will help you figure out more precisely what you are feeling, how intensely you're feeling it, how long it lasts, and why you might be feeling this way. This will empower you to find positive ways to put that information to use.

There is no set schedule for what day to start or how long it should take to finish all the prompts, but if you can commit to journaling about your emotions at least a few times a week, you are likely to experience the benefits of mindfulness.

Here's how to do it:

1. Find a safe and comfortable place to sit where you can focus.

2. Take five deep, slow breaths, counting to four on the inhale and to eight on the exhale. (When you exhale slowly, it helps your body relax.)

3. Decide to explore how you are feeling in the moment or to examine a recent feeling.

4. Read through the list of feelings and sensations and select those that most accurately represent what you are/were feeling. If this brings up discomfort, try not to get distracted or panicky. Instead, repeat the breathing exercise from Step 2, concentrating on relaxing through your long, slow exhalation.

5. When you are ready, write down the feelings and sensations you identified. Follow the prompts, stopping to breathe if you feel tense or overwhelmed. Feel free to stand up, stretch, walk, or move in other ways that feel good.

6. Remember not to judge your feelings. Just keep noticing and naming them.

Note that people who have experienced trauma may find this exercise particularly difficult. Sometimes trauma leaves us feeling numb, unable to connect with ourselves; alternatively, it can cause intense discomfort. In the latter case, please stop and seek help immediately—ask someone close to you whom you trust for support, or reach out to a mental health help line (see page 174 for resources) right away.

Practicing these steps on a regular basis is a great way to get better at identifying your feelings and describing them accurately. You will develop your personal vocabulary of feeling. Over time, you can gain a sense of your own emotional landscape—how you typically react to the world around you, how you handle challenging feelings, what your reactions tend to be, and how you can thoughtfully respond to situations. Eventually you may find you have made a habit of checking in with yourself regularly, keeping track of how you feel, being in the moment—and you will have incorporated the practice of mindfulness into your daily life.

The Feelings List

The lists that follow, while not comprehensive, include a lot of words to describe how you might be feeling. We wanted to provide many options so you can be as accurate as possible about what you are experiencing. Many of the words are similar, or even synonymous—but rather than being repetitious, the idea is to allow you to choose the word that you feel most specifically captures how you are feeling in a particular moment. Feel free to add your own words in the spaces provided.

Physical or Bodily Sensations

These are sensations that you may feel in your body. Sometimes we notice these first—they provide insight into how we are feeling emotionally, but they do not encompass all that we are feeling.

Achy	Churning	Dry	Glowing
Alive	Clammy	Dull	Glutted
Antsy	Clenched	Dyspeptic	Goose bumps
Aroused	Cold	Electrified	Gurgling
Athletic	Contractions	Energetic	Hallucinating
Battered	Congested	Faint	Heart pounding
Beaten	Constipated	Famished	Heaviness
Bleeding	Constricted	Feverish	High
Bloated	Cool	Fidgety	Hollowed out
Blocked	Cozy	Floating	Horny
Blushing	Cramped	Flowing	Hot
Breathless	Cramping	Fluid	Hungover
Bruised	Craving	Flushed	Hungry
Burning	Crying	Fluttery	Hurting
Butterflies in stomach	Delirious	Frozen	Icy
	Diarrhea	Full stomach	Ill
Buzzing	Dizzy	Fullness	Impaired
Chilled	Drained	Gassy	In pain
Choking	Drunk	Giddy	Incapacitated

Intoxicated	Pins and needles	Short of breath	Stuffed up
Itchy	Poisoned	Slack	Stuttering
Jonesing	Pressed	Sleepy	Suffocated
Knotted	Prickly	Slow	Sweaty
Light	Pulsing	Sluggish	Tender
Light-headed	Pummeled	Smooth	Tense
Limp	Pushed	Smothered	Thirsty
Loose	Quaking	Sneezing	Throbbing
Lump in throat	Queasy	Sniffling	Ticklish
Lusting	Radiating	Snug	Tickly
Melting	Rained on	Soft	Tight
Moist	Releasing	Sore	Tingling
Molested	Rigid	Spent	Trembling
Nauseated	Run-down	Squeamish	Twitching
Off-balance	Salivating	Squished	Uncomfortable
On fire	Sated	Starving	Vibrating
Orgasmic	Scarred	Stiff	Vomiting
Oversensitive	Sedated	Still	Warm
Palpitations	Sensitized	Stomachache	Weak
Pangs	Sensual	Stoned	Wet
Panting	Shaking	Straining	Wiped out
Peckish	Shaky	Strong	Wobbly
Perspiring	Shivery	Stuffed	Wooden

_____

_____

_____

_____

_____

_____

Emotions and Feelings

These are your mind's interpretation of what you are experiencing. These feelings may be partially based on physical sensations, but they also incorporate influences such as context, past experiences, hopes for or concerns about the future, facts and knowledge, personal narratives, and other factors.

Absorbed	Amorous	Bereaved	Challenged
Abused	Amused	Besotted	Charmed
Accepting	Angry	Betrayed	Cheeky
Addicted	Angsty	Betraying	Cheerful
Adequate	Anguished	Bewildered	Cheerless
Admired	Annoyed	Bitter	Clueless
Admiring	Anticipating	Blah	Coerced
Adored	Anxious	Blamed	Coercive
Adoring	Apathetic	Blank	Comfortable
Adventurous	Appreciated	Bleak	Compassionate
Affectionate	Appreciative	Blessed	Competent
Affronted	Apprehensive	Blissful	Complacent
Afraid	Ashamed	Blue	Complete
Aggravated	Astonished	Bold	Composed
Aggressive	Attached	Bored	Concerned
Aghast	Attracted	Brave	Condescended to
Agitated	Averse	Broken	Condescending
Agonized	Awestruck	Bubbly	Confident
Aimless	Awful	Bullied	Confrontational
Alarmed	Awkward	Bummed out	Confused
Alert	Baffled	Burned-out	Connected
Alienated	Bashful	Calm	Consoled
Alive	Battered	Capable	Contemplative
Alone	Beaten down	Cared for	Contemptuous
Aloof	Beautiful	Carefree	Content
Amazed	Belittled	Caring	Controlled
Ambivalent	Bemused	Centered	Controlling

Courageous	Depleted	Distraught	Energized
Cowardly	Depressed	Distressed	Engaged
Cowed	Deprived	Distrusted	Enraged
Crabby	Desired	Distrustful	Enthralled
Cranky	Desirous	Disturbed	Enthusiastic
Creative	Despairing	Dominant	Envious
Critical	Desperate	Dominated	Euphoric
Criticized	Despondent	Doomed	Evasive
Cruel	Detached	Doting	Evil
Crushed	Determined	Doubted	Exasperated
Curious	Devastated	Doubtful	Excited
Cynical	Devoted	Downhearted	Exhausted
Damaged	Diminished	Downtrodden	Exhilarated
Dangerous	Dirty	Dreadful	Expectant
Daring	Disappointed	Dreading	Exploited
Daunted	Disapproving	Dreamy	Exploring
Dazzled	Disconnected	Dutiful	Exposed
Debilitated	Discontent	Eager	Fabulous
Decadent	Discouraged	Easy like Sunday morning	False
Deceitful	Disdainful	Ecstatic	Fascinated
Deceived	Disenchanted	Elated	Fascinating
Dedicated	Disgruntled	Embarrassed	Fearful
Defeated	Disgusted	Embattled	Fearless
Defenseless	Dishonored	Embittered	Fed up
Defensive	Disillusioned	Emboldened	Ferocious
Defiant	Disinterested	Emotional	Festive
Deficient	Dismayed	Emotionless	Fierce
Deflated	Dismissed	Empathetic	Fixated
Degraded	Displeased	Empowered	Flighty
Dejected	Disrespected	Empty	Flirtatious
Delicate	Dissatisfied	Enchanted	Floored
Delighted	Distant	Encouraged	Floundering
Demoralized	Distracted		Flourishing

Flustered	Gloomy	Homesick	Interested
Focused	Glowing	Honored	Intimidated
Foggy brained	Glum	Hopeful	Intimidating
Foolish	Gonzo	Hopeless	Intrigued
Forgiven	Graced	Hormonal	Introspective
Forgiving	Grateful	Horrified	Invalidated
Forgotten	Grave	Hostile	Invigorated
Forlorn	Grieving	Humbled	Invincible
Forsaken	Grossed out	Humiliated	Invisible
Fortunate	Grouchy	Hurt	Involved
Fragile	Grounded	Hyper	Irate
Fraudulent	Guarded	Idiotic	Irrational
Frazzled	Guilty	Ignored	Irrelevant
Freaked-out	Gutted	Ill at ease	Irresistible
Free	Hangry	Impatient	Irritable
Frenzied	Hapless	Imperfect	Irritated
Fretful	Happy	Impotent	Isolated
Friendless	Harassed	Impressed	Jaded
Friendly	Harmonious	Impulsive	Jealous
Frightened	Harried	In control	Jovial
Frisky	Hated	Inadequate	Joyful
Frolicsome	Hating	Incensed	Joyless
Frustrated	Healed	Indecisive	Jubilant
Fulfilled	Healthy	Indifferent	Judged
Fuming	Heard	Indignant	Judgmental
Furious	Heartbroken	Infatuated	Jumpy
Fussy	Heartsick	Inferior	Kind
Game	Helped	Inhibited	Known
Generous	Helpful	Innocent	Laid-back
Gentle	Helpless	Insane	Languid
Genuine	Heroic	Insecure	Lethargic
Giving	Hesitant	Inspired	Likable
Gleeful	High-spirited	Insulted	Listless

Lively	Mystified	Over it	Poised
Livid	Nasty	Overcome	Popular
Loathsome	Natural	Overjoyed	Powerful
Lonely	Needed	Overwhelmed	Powerless
Longing	Needy	Overworked	Pragmatic
Lost	Negative	Pained	Preoccupied
Lovable	Neglected	Pampered	Present
Loved	Nervous	Panicky	Preyed upon
Loveless	Neutral	Paralyzed	Privileged
Loving	Noncommittal	Paranoid	Prized
Low	Nostalgic	Passionate	Productive
Luckless	Numb	Passive	Professional
Lucky	Nurtured	Patient	Protected
Lustful	Nurturing	Patronized	Protective
Mad	Obedient	Peaceful	Proud
Manic	Objectified	Peeved	Provocative
Mean	Obligated	Peevish	Provoked
Meek	Obliging	Pensive	Pure
Melancholy	Obsessed	Perfectionistic	Purposeful
Mellow	Offended	Perky	Pushy
Merry	Old	Perplexed	Put down
Mischievous	On edge	Persecuted	Puzzled
Miserable	Open	Persuasive	Qualified
Mistreated	Opposed	Petrified	Quarrelsome
Mistrustful	Oppressed	Petty	Questioned
Mixed-up	Optimistic	Petulant	Questioning
Mocked	Ostracized	Phony	Quiet
Moody	Out of balance	Pissed off	Radiant
Mortified	Out of control	Pitied	Radical
Morose	Out of place	Pitiful	Rattled
Mournful	Outdated	Placid	Raw
Moved	Outgoing	Playful	Reactive
Mutinous	Outraged	Pleased	Ready

Reassured	Resourceful	Scared	Shut down
Rebellious	Respected	Scarred	Shut out
Rebuffed	Respectful	Scattered	Shy
Rebuked	Responsible	Secure	Sickened
Recalcitrant	Rested	Seduced	Silenced
Receptive	Restless	Seductive	Silly
Reckless	Reverent	Self-absorbed	Sincere
Reclusive	Revitalized	Self-accepting	Skeptical
Reconciled	Revolted	Self-assured	Smart
Reenergized	Ridiculed	Self-confident	Smitten
Reflective	Ridiculing	Self-conscious	Smug
Refreshed	Ridiculous	Self-critical	Sneaky
Regretful	Robotic	Self-deprecating	Snubbed
Rejected	Robust	Self-disciplined	Sociable
Rejecting	Romantic	Self-loving	Solemn
Rejoicing	Rotten	Self-reliant	Somber
Rejuvenated	Ruined	Self-sacrificing	Soothed
Relaxed	Rushed	Selfish	Sorrowful
Released	Ruthless	Selfless	Sorry
Relieved	Sabotaged	Sensible	Sour
Reluctant	Sacrificed	Sensitive	Spacey
Remorseful	Sad	Serene	Sparkling
Renewed	Sadistic	Settled	Special
Repentant	Safe	Sexy	Speechless
Replenished	Sane	Shaken	Spiteful
Rescued	Sanguine	Shallow	Spontaneous
Resentful	Sarcastic	Shamed	Spooked
Reserved	Sassy	Shameful	Stable
Resigned	Sated	Sheepish	Stale
Resilient	Satisfied	Shocked	Startled
Resistant	Scandalized	Shortchanged	Stereotyped
Resolved	Scandalous	Shot down	Stern

Stimulated	Suspicious	Traumatized	Vain
Stingy	Sweet	Tricked	Valiant
Stoic	Sympathetic	Triggered	Vengeful
Strange	Talkative	Triumphant	Vibrant
Stressed	Talked out	Trusting	Victimized
Stretched	Tearful	Turbulent	Vindictive
Stricken	Tender	Ugly	Vulnerable
Strong	Tense	Unappreciated	Warm
Stubborn	Terrified	Uncomfortable	Weak
Stuck	Testy	Undecided	Weary
Stumped	Thankful	Understanding	Well
Stunned	Thoughtful	Undone	Willful
Stupid	Threatened	Uneasy	Wise
Stylish	Thrilled	Unforgiving	Withdrawn
Suicidal	Tickled	Unhappy	Woeful
Sullen	Timid	Unsettled	Wonderful
Sunny	Tolerant	Unsure	Worn-out
Superior	Tolerated	Untrustworthy	Worried
Superstitious	Torn	Upbeat	Worthless
Supported	Touched	Upset	Worthy
Supportive	Touchy	Used	Wretched
Surly	Tranquil	Useful	Yearning
Surprised	Trapped	Useless	Zen

_____

_____

_____

_____

_____

Journaling
Prompts

Date: .... *Time:* ....

Right now I am feeling (list all the feelings and sensations that apply):

....

....

....

....

....

....

....

A word from the Feelings List on page 12 or a short sentence that best describes the state I'm in or what I am experiencing:

....

....

Intensity of this feeling:

low-key   real   fierce

How my body feels:

....

....

....

....

....

Are there any visual images I associate with this feeling? If so, draw or color below:

Is there a song or a piece of music that reflects this feeling?

....

Would I describe the feeling as positive, neutral, or negative? Why?

....

....

....

What do I think caused or influenced this feeling?

....

....

....

....

Does this feeling bring up anything from my past?

....

....

....

....

Is this feeling uncomfortable in any way? If so, how?

....

....

....

....

Am I tempted to judge this feeling? Can I pause and just be with it? How does that feel?

....

....

....

....

Does this feeling cause an urge to perform any actions or behaviors? If so, what are they? Can I explain why? Are these positive responses?

....

....

....

....

....

How long did this feeling last?

....

When this feeling started

|

When it ended

Did this feeling appear and disappear gradually or abruptly?

....

Do I expect to feel this way again?

....

Any other notes I want to add about this feeling:

....

....

....

....

....

....

Date: .... *Time:* ....

Right now I am feeling (list all the feelings and sensations that apply):

....

....

....

....

....

....

....

A word from the Feelings List on page 12 or a short sentence that best describes
the state I'm in or what I am experiencing:

....

....

Intensity of this feeling:

low-key   real   fierce

How my body feels:

....

....

....

....

....

Are there any visual images I associate with this feeling? If so, draw or color below:

Is there a song or a piece of music that reflects this feeling?

....

Would I describe the feeling as positive, neutral, or negative? Why?

....

....

....

What do I think caused or influenced this feeling?

....

....

....

....

Does this feeling bring up anything from my past?

....

....

....

....

Is this feeling uncomfortable in any way? If so, how?

....

....

....

....

Am I tempted to judge this feeling? Can I pause and just be with it? How does that feel?

....

....

....

....

Does this feeling cause an urge to perform any actions or behaviors? If so, what are they? Can I explain why? Are these positive responses?

....

....

....

....

....

How long did this feeling last?

....

When this feeling started

|

When it ended

Did this feeling appear and disappear gradually or abruptly?

....

Do I expect to feel this way again?

....

Any other notes I want to add about this feeling:

....

....

....

....

....

....

Date: .... Time: ....

Right now I am feeling (list all the feelings and sensations that apply):

....

....

....

....

....

....

....

A word from the Feelings List on page 12 or a short sentence that best describes
the state I'm in or what I am experiencing:

....

....

Intensity of this feeling:

low-key   real   fierce

How my body feels:

....

....

....

....

....

Are there any visual images I associate with this feeling? If so, draw or color below:

Is there a song or a piece of music that reflects this feeling?

....

Would I describe the feeling as positive, neutral, or negative? Why?

....

....

....

What do I think caused or influenced this feeling?

....

....

....

....

Does this feeling bring up anything from my past?

....

....

....

....

Is this feeling uncomfortable in any way? If so, how?

....

....

....

....

Am I tempted to judge this feeling? Can I pause and just be with it? How does that feel?

....

....

....

....

Does this feeling cause an urge to perform any actions or behaviors? If so, what are they? Can I explain why? Are these positive responses?

....

....

....

....

....

How long did this feeling last?

....

When this feeling started

|

When it ended

Did this feeling appear and disappear gradually or abruptly?

....

Do I expect to feel this way again?

....

Any other notes I want to add about this feeling:

....

....

....

....

....

....

Date: .... *Time:* ....

Right now I am feeling (list all the feelings and sensations that apply):

....

....

....

....

....

....

....

A word from the Feelings List on page 12 or a short sentence that best describes
the state I'm in or what I am experiencing:

....

....

Intensity of this feeling:

low-key   real   fierce

How my body feels:

....

....

....

....

....

Are there any visual images I associate with this feeling? If so, draw or color below:

Is there a song or a piece of music that reflects this feeling?

....

Would I describe the feeling as positive, neutral, or negative? Why?

....

....

....

What do I think caused or influenced this feeling?

....

....

....

....

Does this feeling bring up anything from my past?

....

....

....

....

Is this feeling uncomfortable in any way? If so, how?

....

....

....

....

Am I tempted to judge this feeling? Can I pause and just be with it? How does that feel?

....

....

....

....

Does this feeling cause an urge to perform any actions or behaviors? If so, what are they? Can I explain why? Are these positive responses?

....

....

....

....

....

How long did this feeling last?

....

When this feeling started

When it ended

Did this feeling appear and disappear gradually or abruptly?

....

Do I expect to feel this way again?

....

Any other notes I want to add about this feeling:

....

....

....

....

....

....

Date: .... *Time:* ....

Right now I am feeling (list all the feelings and sensations that apply):

....

....

....

....

....

....

....

A word from the Feelings List on page 12 or a short sentence that best describes
the state I'm in or what I am experiencing:

....

....

Intensity of this feeling:

low-key   real   fierce

How my body feels:

....

....

....

....

....

Are there any visual images I associate with this feeling? If so, draw or color below:

Is there a song or a piece of music that reflects this feeling?

....

Would I describe the feeling as positive, neutral, or negative? Why?

....

....

....

What do I think caused or influenced this feeling?

....

....

....

....

Does this feeling bring up anything from my past?

....
....
....
....

Is this feeling uncomfortable in any way? If so, how?

....
....
....
....

Am I tempted to judge this feeling? Can I pause and just be with it? How does that feel?

....
....
....
....

Does this feeling cause an urge to perform any actions or behaviors? If so, what are they? Can I explain why? Are these positive responses?

....
....
....
....
....

How long did this feeling last?

....

When this feeling started

|

When it ended

Did this feeling appear and disappear gradually or abruptly?

....

Do I expect to feel this way again?

....

Any other notes I want to add about this feeling:

....

....

....

....

....

....

Date: .... *Time:* ....

Right now I am feeling (list all the feelings and sensations that apply):

....

....

....

....

....

....

....

A word from the Feelings List on page 12 or a short sentence that best describes
the state I'm in or what I am experiencing:

....

....

Intensity of this feeling:

low-key   real   fierce

How my body feels:

....

....

....

....

....

Are there any visual images I associate with this feeling? If so, draw or color below:

Is there a song or a piece of music that reflects this feeling?

....

Would I describe the feeling as positive, neutral, or negative? Why?

....

....

....

What do I think caused or influenced this feeling?

....

....

....

....

Does this feeling bring up anything from my past?

....

....

....

....

Is this feeling uncomfortable in any way? If so, how?

....

....

....

....

Am I tempted to judge this feeling? Can I pause and just be with it? How does that feel?

....

....

....

....

Does this feeling cause an urge to perform any actions or behaviors? If so, what are they? Can I explain why? Are these positive responses?

....

....

....

....

....

How long did this feeling last?

....

When this feeling started

|

When it ended

Did this feeling appear and disappear gradually or abruptly?

....

Do I expect to feel this way again?

....

Any other notes I want to add about this feeling:

....

....

....

....

....

....

Date: .... Time: ....

Right now I am feeling (list all the feelings and sensations that apply):

....

....

....

....

....

....

....

A word from the Feelings List on page 12 or a short sentence that best describes
the state I'm in or what I am experiencing:

....

....

Intensity of this feeling:

low-key				real				fierce

How my body feels:

....

....

....

....

....

Are there any visual images I associate with this feeling? If so, draw or color below:

Is there a song or a piece of music that reflects this feeling?

....

Would I describe the feeling as positive, neutral, or negative? Why?

....

....

....

What do I think caused or influenced this feeling?

....

....

....

....

Does this feeling bring up anything from my past?

....

....

....

....

Is this feeling uncomfortable in any way? If so, how?

....

....

....

....

Am I tempted to judge this feeling? Can I pause and just be with it? How does that feel?

....

....

....

....

Does this feeling cause an urge to perform any actions or behaviors? If so, what are they? Can I explain why? Are these positive responses?

....

....

....

....

....

How long did this feeling last?

....

When this feeling started

When it ended

Did this feeling appear and disappear gradually or abruptly?

....

Do I expect to feel this way again?

....

Any other notes I want to add about this feeling:

....

....

....

....

....

....

Date: .... *Time:* ....

Right now I am feeling (list all the feelings and sensations that apply):

....

....

....

....

....

....

....

A word from the Feelings List on page 12 or a short sentence that best describes the state I'm in or what I am experiencing:

....

....

Intensity of this feeling:

low-key				real				fierce

How my body feels:

....

....

....

....

....

Are there any visual images I associate with this feeling? If so, draw or color below:

Is there a song or a piece of music that reflects this feeling?

....

Would I describe the feeling as positive, neutral, or negative? Why?

....

....

....

What do I think caused or influenced this feeling?

....

....

....

....

Does this feeling bring up anything from my past?

....

....

....

....

Is this feeling uncomfortable in any way? If so, how?

....

....

....

....

Am I tempted to judge this feeling? Can I pause and just be with it? How does that feel?

....

....

....

....

Does this feeling cause an urge to perform any actions or behaviors? If so, what are they? Can I explain why? Are these positive responses?

....

....

....

....

....

How long did this feeling last?

....

When this feeling started

|

When it ended

Did this feeling appear and disappear gradually or abruptly?

....

Do I expect to feel this way again?

....

Any other notes I want to add about this feeling:

....

....

....

....

....

....

Date: .... *Time:* ....

Right now I am feeling (list all the feelings and sensations that apply):

....

....

....

....

....

....

....

A word from the Feelings List on page 12 or a short sentence that best describes the state I'm in or what I am experiencing:

....

....

Intensity of this feeling:

low-key   real   fierce

How my body feels:

....

....

....

....

....

Are there any visual images I associate with this feeling? If so, draw or color below:

Is there a song or a piece of music that reflects this feeling?

....

Would I describe the feeling as positive, neutral, or negative? Why?

....

....

....

What do I think caused or influenced this feeling?

....

....

....

....

Does this feeling bring up anything from my past?

....

....

....

....

Is this feeling uncomfortable in any way? If so, how?

....

....

....

....

Am I tempted to judge this feeling? Can I pause and just be with it? How does that feel?

....

....

....

....

Does this feeling cause an urge to perform any actions or behaviors? If so, what are they? Can I explain why? Are these positive responses?

....

....

....

....

....

How long did this feeling last?

....

When this feeling started

|

When it ended

Did this feeling appear and disappear gradually or abruptly?

....

Do I expect to feel this way again?

....

Any other notes I want to add about this feeling:

....

....

....

....

....

....

Date: .... Time: ....

Right now I am feeling (list all the feelings and sensations that apply):

....

....

....

....

....

....

....

A word from the Feelings List on page 12 or a short sentence that best describes the state I'm in or what I am experiencing:

....

....

Intensity of this feeling:

low-key   real   fierce

How my body feels:

....

....

....

....

....

Are there any visual images I associate with this feeling? If so, draw or color below:

Is there a song or a piece of music that reflects this feeling?

....

Would I describe the feeling as positive, neutral, or negative? Why?

....

....

....

What do I think caused or influenced this feeling?

....

....

....

....

Does this feeling bring up anything from my past?

....

....

....

....

Is this feeling uncomfortable in any way? If so, how?

....

....

....

....

Am I tempted to judge this feeling? Can I pause and just be with it? How does that feel?

....

....

....

....

Does this feeling cause an urge to perform any actions or behaviors? If so, what are they? Can I explain why? Are these positive responses?

....

....

....

....

....

How long did this feeling last?

....

When this feeling started

When it ended

Did this feeling appear and disappear gradually or abruptly?

....

Do I expect to feel this way again?

....

Any other notes I want to add about this feeling:

....

....

....

....

....

....

Date: .... *Time:* ....

Right now I am feeling (list all the feelings and sensations that apply):

....

....

....

....

....

....

....

A word from the Feelings List on page 12 or a short sentence that best describes the state I'm in or what I am experiencing:

....

....

Intensity of this feeling:

low-key   real   fierce

How my body feels:

....

....

....

....

....

Are there any visual images I associate with this feeling? If so, draw or color below:

Is there a song or a piece of music that reflects this feeling?

....

Would I describe the feeling as positive, neutral, or negative? Why?

....

....

....

What do I think caused or influenced this feeling?

....

....

....

....

Does this feeling bring up anything from my past?

....

....

....

....

Is this feeling uncomfortable in any way? If so, how?

....

....

....

....

Am I tempted to judge this feeling? Can I pause and just be with it? How does that feel?

....

....

....

....

Does this feeling cause an urge to perform any actions or behaviors? If so, what are they? Can I explain why? Are these positive responses?

....

....

....

....

....

How long did this feeling last?

....

When this feeling started

When it ended

Did this feeling appear and disappear gradually or abruptly?

....

Do I expect to feel this way again?

....

Any other notes I want to add about this feeling:

....

....

....

....

....

....

Date: .... *Time:* ....

Right now I am feeling (list all the feelings and sensations that apply):

....

....

....

....

....

....

....

A word from the Feelings List on page 12 or a short sentence that best describes the state I'm in or what I am experiencing:

....

....

Intensity of this feeling:

low-key				real				fierce

How my body feels:

....

....

....

....

....

Are there any visual images I associate with this feeling? If so, draw or color below:

Is there a song or a piece of music that reflects this feeling?

....

Would I describe the feeling as positive, neutral, or negative? Why?

....

....

....

What do I think caused or influenced this feeling?

....

....

....

....

Does this feeling bring up anything from my past?

....

....

....

....

Is this feeling uncomfortable in any way? If so, how?

....

....

....

....

Am I tempted to judge this feeling? Can I pause and just be with it? How does that feel?

....

....

....

....

Does this feeling cause an urge to perform any actions or behaviors? If so, what are they? Can I explain why? Are these positive responses?

....

....

....

....

....

How long did this feeling last?

....

When this feeling started

|

When it ended

Did this feeling appear and disappear gradually or abruptly?

....

Do I expect to feel this way again?

....

Any other notes I want to add about this feeling:

....

....

....

....

....

....

Date: .... *Time:* ....

Right now I am feeling (list all the feelings and sensations that apply):

....

....

....

....

....

....

....

A word from the Feelings List on page 12 or a short sentence that best describes the state I'm in or what I am experiencing:

....

....

Intensity of this feeling:

low-key   real   fierce

How my body feels:

....

....

....

....

....

Are there any visual images I associate with this feeling? If so, draw or color below:

Is there a song or a piece of music that reflects this feeling?

....

Would I describe the feeling as positive, neutral, or negative? Why?

....

....

....

What do I think caused or influenced this feeling?

....

....

....

....

Does this feeling bring up anything from my past?

....

....

....

....

Is this feeling uncomfortable in any way? If so, how?

....

....

....

....

Am I tempted to judge this feeling? Can I pause and just be with it? How does that feel?

....

....

....

....

Does this feeling cause an urge to perform any actions or behaviors? If so, what are they? Can I explain why? Are these positive responses?

....

....

....

....

....

How long did this feeling last?

....

When this feeling started

|

When it ended

Did this feeling appear and disappear gradually or abruptly?

....

Do I expect to feel this way again?

....

Any other notes I want to add about this feeling:

....

....

....

....

....

....

Date:...   Time:.................................

Right now I am feeling (list all the feelings and sensations that apply):

....

....

....

....

....

....

....

A word from the Feelings List on page 12 or a short sentence that best describes
the state I'm in or what I am experiencing:

....

....

Intensity of this feeling:

| | | | | | | | |
low-key   real   fierce

How my body feels:

....

....

....

....

....

Are there any visual images I associate with this feeling? If so, draw or color below:

Is there a song or a piece of music that reflects this feeling?

....

Would I describe the feeling as positive, neutral, or negative? Why?

....

....

....

What do I think caused or influenced this feeling?

....

....

....

....

Does this feeling bring up anything from my past?

....
....
....
....

Is this feeling uncomfortable in any way? If so, how?

....
....
....
....

Am I tempted to judge this feeling? Can I pause and just be with it? How does that feel?

....
....
....
....

Does this feeling cause an urge to perform any actions or behaviors? If so, what are they? Can I explain why? Are these positive responses?

....
....
....
....
....

How long did this feeling last?

....

When this feeling started

When it ended

Did this feeling appear and disappear gradually or abruptly?

....

Do I expect to feel this way again?

....

Any other notes I want to add about this feeling:

....

....

....

....

....

....

Date: .... Time: ....

Right now I am feeling (list all the feelings and sensations that apply):

....

....

....

....

....

....

....

A word from the Feelings List on page 12 or a short sentence that best describes
the state I'm in or what I am experiencing:

....

....

Intensity of this feeling:

low-key   real   fierce

How my body feels:

....

....

....

....

....

Are there any visual images I associate with this feeling? If so, draw or color below:

Is there a song or a piece of music that reflects this feeling?

....

Would I describe the feeling as positive, neutral, or negative? Why?

....

....

....

What do I think caused or influenced this feeling?

....

....

....

....

Does this feeling bring up anything from my past?

....

....

....

....

Is this feeling uncomfortable in any way? If so, how?

....

....

....

....

Am I tempted to judge this feeling? Can I pause and just be with it? How does that feel?

....

....

....

....

Does this feeling cause an urge to perform any actions or behaviors? If so, what are they? Can I explain why? Are these positive responses?

....

....

....

....

....

How long did this feeling last?

....

When this feeling started

When it ended

Did this feeling appear and disappear gradually or abruptly?

....

Do I expect to feel this way again?

....

Any other notes I want to add about this feeling:

....

....

....

....

....

....

Date:... *Time:*...................................

Right now I am feeling (list all the feelings and sensations that apply):

....

....

....

....

....

....

....

A word from the Feelings List on page 12 or a short sentence that best describes
the state I'm in or what I am experiencing:

....

....

Intensity of this feeling:

low-key   real   fierce

How my body feels:

....

....

....

....

....

Are there any visual images I associate with this feeling? If so, draw or color below:

Is there a song or a piece of music that reflects this feeling?

....

Would I describe the feeling as positive, neutral, or negative? Why?

....

....

....

What do I think caused or influenced this feeling?

....

....

....

....

Does this feeling bring up anything from my past?

....

....

....

....

Is this feeling uncomfortable in any way? If so, how?

....

....

....

....

Am I tempted to judge this feeling? Can I pause and just be with it? How does that feel?

....

....

....

....

Does this feeling cause an urge to perform any actions or behaviors? If so, what are they? Can I explain why? Are these positive responses?

....

....

....

....

....

How long did this feeling last?

....

When this feeling started

|

When it ended

Did this feeling appear and disappear gradually or abruptly?

....

Do I expect to feel this way again?

....

Any other notes I want to add about this feeling:

....

....

....

....

....

....

Date:... Time:...............................

Right now I am feeling (list all the feelings and sensations that apply):

....

....

....

....

....

....

....

A word from the Feelings List on page 12 or a short sentence that best describes
the state I'm in or what I am experiencing:

....

....

Intensity of this feeling:

low-key				real				fierce

How my body feels:

....

....

....

....

....

Are there any visual images I associate with this feeling? If so, draw or color below:

Is there a song or a piece of music that reflects this feeling?

....

Would I describe the feeling as positive, neutral, or negative? Why?

....

....

....

What do I think caused or influenced this feeling?

....

....

....

....

Does this feeling bring up anything from my past?

....

....

....

....

Is this feeling uncomfortable in any way? If so, how?

....

....

....

....

Am I tempted to judge this feeling? Can I pause and just be with it? How does that feel?

....

....

....

....

Does this feeling cause an urge to perform any actions or behaviors? If so, what are they? Can I explain why? Are these positive responses?

....

....

....

....

....

How long did this feeling last?

....

When this feeling started

|

When it ended

Did this feeling appear and disappear gradually or abruptly?

....

Do I expect to feel this way again?

....

Any other notes I want to add about this feeling:

....

....

....

....

....

....

Date:... *Time:*................................

Right now I am feeling (list all the feelings and sensations that apply):

....

....

....

....

....

....

....

A word from the Feelings List on page 12 or a short sentence that best describes
the state I'm in or what I am experiencing:

....

....

Intensity of this feeling:

low-key   real   fierce

How my body feels:

....

....

....

....

....

Are there any visual images I associate with this feeling? If so, draw or color below:

Is there a song or a piece of music that reflects this feeling?

....

Would I describe the feeling as positive, neutral, or negative? Why?

....

....

....

What do I think caused or influenced this feeling?

....

....

....

....

Does this feeling bring up anything from my past?

....

....

....

....

Is this feeling uncomfortable in any way? If so, how?

....

....

....

....

Am I tempted to judge this feeling? Can I pause and just be with it? How does that feel?

....

....

....

....

Does this feeling cause an urge to perform any actions or behaviors? If so, what are they? Can I explain why? Are these positive responses?

....

....

....

....

....

How long did this feeling last?

....

When this feeling started

|

|

|

|

When it ended

Did this feeling appear and disappear gradually or abruptly?

....

Do I expect to feel this way again?

....

Any other notes I want to add about this feeling:

....

....

....

....

....

....

Date: .... *Time:* ....

Right now I am feeling (list all the feelings and sensations that apply):

....

....

....

....

....

....

....

A word from the Feelings List on page 12 or a short sentence that best describes the state I'm in or what I am experiencing:

....

....

Intensity of this feeling:

low-key   real   fierce

How my body feels:

....

....

....

....

....

Are there any visual images I associate with this feeling? If so, draw or color below:

Is there a song or a piece of music that reflects this feeling?

....

Would I describe the feeling as positive, neutral, or negative? Why?

....

....

....

What do I think caused or influenced this feeling?

....

....

....

....

Does this feeling bring up anything from my past?

....

....

....

....

Is this feeling uncomfortable in any way? If so, how?

....

....

....

....

Am I tempted to judge this feeling? Can I pause and just be with it? How does that feel?

....

....

....

....

Does this feeling cause an urge to perform any actions or behaviors? If so, what are they? Can I explain why? Are these positive responses?

....

....

....

....

....

How long did this feeling last?

....

When this feeling started

When it ended

Did this feeling appear and disappear gradually or abruptly?

....

Do I expect to feel this way again?

....

Any other notes I want to add about this feeling:

....

....

....

....

....

....

Date:.. *Time:* ....

Right now I am feeling (list all the feelings and sensations that apply):

....

....

....

....

....

....

....

A word from the Feelings List on page 12 or a short sentence that best describes
the state I'm in or what I am experiencing:

....

....

Intensity of this feeling:

low-key   real   fierce

How my body feels:

....

....

....

....

....

Are there any visual images I associate with this feeling? If so, draw or color below:

Is there a song or a piece of music that reflects this feeling?

....

Would I describe the feeling as positive, neutral, or negative? Why?

....

....

....

What do I think caused or influenced this feeling?

....

....

....

....

Does this feeling bring up anything from my past?

....

....

....

....

Is this feeling uncomfortable in any way? If so, how?

....

....

....

....

Am I tempted to judge this feeling? Can I pause and just be with it? How does that feel?

....

....

....

....

Does this feeling cause an urge to perform any actions or behaviors? If so, what are they? Can I explain why? Are these positive responses?

....

....

....

....

....

How long did this feeling last?

....

When this feeling started

|

When it ended

Did this feeling appear and disappear gradually or abruptly?

....

Do I expect to feel this way again?

....

Any other notes I want to add about this feeling:

....

....

....

....

....

....

Date: .... *Time:* ....

Right now I am feeling (list all the feelings and sensations that apply):

....

....

....

....

....

....

....

A word from the Feelings List on page 12 or a short sentence that best describes the state I'm in or what I am experiencing:

....

....

Intensity of this feeling:

low-key				real			fierce

How my body feels:

....

....

....

....

....

Are there any visual images I associate with this feeling? If so, draw or color below:

Is there a song or a piece of music that reflects this feeling?

....

Would I describe the feeling as positive, neutral, or negative? Why?

....

....

....

What do I think caused or influenced this feeling?

....

....

....

....

Does this feeling bring up anything from my past?

....

....

....

....

Is this feeling uncomfortable in any way? If so, how?

....

....

....

....

Am I tempted to judge this feeling? Can I pause and just be with it? How does that feel?

....

....

....

....

Does this feeling cause an urge to perform any actions or behaviors? If so, what are they? Can I explain why? Are these positive responses?

....

....

....

....

....

How long did this feeling last?

....

When this feeling started

When it ended

Did this feeling appear and disappear gradually or abruptly?

....

Do I expect to feel this way again?

....

Any other notes I want to add about this feeling:

....

....

....

....

....

....

Date: .... Time: ....

Right now I am feeling (list all the feelings and sensations that apply):

....

....

....

....

....

....

....

A word from the Feelings List on page 12 or a short sentence that best describes
the state I'm in or what I am experiencing:

....

....

Intensity of this feeling:

low-key				real				fierce

How my body feels:

....

....

....

....

....

Are there any visual images I associate with this feeling? If so, draw or color below:

Is there a song or a piece of music that reflects this feeling?

....

Would I describe the feeling as positive, neutral, or negative? Why?

....

....

....

What do I think caused or influenced this feeling?

....

....

....

....

Does this feeling bring up anything from my past?

....

....

....

....

Is this feeling uncomfortable in any way? If so, how?

....

....

....

....

Am I tempted to judge this feeling? Can I pause and just be with it? How does that feel?

....

....

....

....

Does this feeling cause an urge to perform any actions or behaviors? If so, what are they? Can I explain why? Are these positive responses?

....

....

....

....

....

How long did this feeling last?

....

When this feeling started

When it ended

Did this feeling appear and disappear gradually or abruptly?

....

Do I expect to feel this way again?

....

Any other notes I want to add about this feeling:

....

....

....

....

....

....

Date: .... *Time:* ....

Right now I am feeling (list all the feelings and sensations that apply):

....

....

....

....

....

....

....

A word from the Feelings List on page 12 or a short sentence that best describes
the state I'm in or what I am experiencing:

....

....

Intensity of this feeling:

low-key   real   fierce

How my body feels:

....

....

....

....

....

Are there any visual images I associate with this feeling? If so, draw or color below:

Is there a song or a piece of music that reflects this feeling?

....

Would I describe the feeling as positive, neutral, or negative? Why?

....

....

....

What do I think caused or influenced this feeling?

....

....

....

....

Does this feeling bring up anything from my past?

....

....

....

....

Is this feeling uncomfortable in any way? If so, how?

....

....

....

....

Am I tempted to judge this feeling? Can I pause and just be with it? How does that feel?

....

....

....

....

Does this feeling cause an urge to perform any actions or behaviors? If so, what are they? Can I explain why? Are these positive responses?

....

....

....

....

....

How long did this feeling last?

....

When this feeling started

When it ended

Did this feeling appear and disappear gradually or abruptly?

....

Do I expect to feel this way again?

....

Any other notes I want to add about this feeling:

....

....

....

....

....

....

Date: .... *Time:* ....

Right now I am feeling (list all the feelings and sensations that apply):

....

....

....

....

....

....

....

A word from the Feelings List on page 12 or a short sentence that best describes the state I'm in or what I am experiencing:

....

....

Intensity of this feeling:

low-key   real   fierce

How my body feels:

....

....

....

....

....

Are there any visual images I associate with this feeling? If so, draw or color below:

Is there a song or a piece of music that reflects this feeling?

....

Would I describe the feeling as positive, neutral, or negative? Why?

....

....

....

What do I think caused or influenced this feeling?

....

....

....

....

Does this feeling bring up anything from my past?

....

....

....

....

Is this feeling uncomfortable in any way? If so, how?

....

....

....

....

Am I tempted to judge this feeling? Can I pause and just be with it? How does that feel?

....

....

....

....

Does this feeling cause an urge to perform any actions or behaviors? If so, what are they? Can I explain why? Are these positive responses?

....

....

....

....

....

How long did this feeling last?

....

When this feeling started

|

When it ended

Did this feeling appear and disappear gradually or abruptly?

....

Do I expect to feel this way again?

....

Any other notes I want to add about this feeling:

....

....

....

....

....

....

Date: .... Time: ....

Right now I am feeling (list all the feelings and sensations that apply):

....

....

....

....

....

....

....

A word from the Feelings List on page 12 or a short sentence that best describes the state I'm in or what I am experiencing:

....

....

Intensity of this feeling:

low-key   real   fierce

How my body feels:

....

....

....

....

....

Are there any visual images I associate with this feeling? If so, draw or color below:

Is there a song or a piece of music that reflects this feeling?

....

Would I describe the feeling as positive, neutral, or negative? Why?

....

....

....

What do I think caused or influenced this feeling?

....

....

....

....

Does this feeling bring up anything from my past?

....

....

....

....

Is this feeling uncomfortable in any way? If so, how?

....

....

....

....

Am I tempted to judge this feeling? Can I pause and just be with it? How does that feel?

....

....

....

....

Does this feeling cause an urge to perform any actions or behaviors? If so, what are they? Can I explain why? Are these positive responses?

....

....

....

....

....

How long did this feeling last?

....

When this feeling started

|

When it ended

Did this feeling appear and disappear gradually or abruptly?

....

Do I expect to feel this way again?

....

Any other notes I want to add about this feeling:

....

....

....

....

....

....

Date: .... *Time:* ....

Right now I am feeling (list all the feelings and sensations that apply):

....

....

....

....

....

....

....

A word from the Feelings List on page 12 or a short sentence that best describes the state I'm in or what I am experiencing:

....

....

Intensity of this feeling:

low-key				real				fierce

How my body feels:

....

....

....

....

....

Are there any visual images I associate with this feeling? If so, draw or color below:

Is there a song or a piece of music that reflects this feeling?

....

Would I describe the feeling as positive, neutral, or negative? Why?

....

....

....

What do I think caused or influenced this feeling?

....

....

....

....

Does this feeling bring up anything from my past?

....

....

....

....

Is this feeling uncomfortable in any way? If so, how?

....

....

....

....

Am I tempted to judge this feeling? Can I pause and just be with it? How does that feel?

....

....

....

....

Does this feeling cause an urge to perform any actions or behaviors? If so, what are they? Can I explain why? Are these positive responses?

....

....

....

....

....

How long did this feeling last?

....

When this feeling started

|

When it ended

Did this feeling appear and disappear gradually or abruptly?

....

Do I expect to feel this way again?

....

Any other notes I want to add about this feeling:

....

....

....

....

....

....

Date: .... *Time:* ....

Right now I am feeling (list all the feelings and sensations that apply):

....

....

....

....

....

....

....

A word from the Feelings List on page 12 or a short sentence that best describes
the state I'm in or what I am experiencing:

....

....

Intensity of this feeling:

low-key   real   fierce

How my body feels:

....

....

....

....

....

Are there any visual images I associate with this feeling? If so, draw or color below:

Is there a song or a piece of music that reflects this feeling?

....

Would I describe the feeling as positive, neutral, or negative? Why?

....

....

....

What do I think caused or influenced this feeling?

....

....

....

....

Does this feeling bring up anything from my past?

....
....
....
....

Is this feeling uncomfortable in any way? If so, how?

....
....
....
....

Am I tempted to judge this feeling? Can I pause and just be with it? How does that feel?

....
....
....
....

Does this feeling cause an urge to perform any actions or behaviors? If so, what are they? Can I explain why? Are these positive responses?

....
....
....
....
....

How long did this feeling last?

....

When this feeling started

|

When it ended

Did this feeling appear and disappear gradually or abruptly?

....

Do I expect to feel this way again?

....

Any other notes I want to add about this feeling:

....

....

....

....

....

....

Date:.. Time:................................

Right now I am feeling (list all the feelings and sensations that apply):

....

....

....

....

....

....

....

A word from the Feelings List on page 12 or a short sentence that best describes the state I'm in or what I am experiencing:

....

....

Intensity of this feeling:

low-key   real   fierce

How my body feels:

....

....

....

....

....

Are there any visual images I associate with this feeling? If so, draw or color below:

Is there a song or a piece of music that reflects this feeling?

....

Would I describe the feeling as positive, neutral, or negative? Why?

....

....

....

What do I think caused or influenced this feeling?

....

....

....

....

Does this feeling bring up anything from my past?

....

....

....

....

Is this feeling uncomfortable in any way? If so, how?

....

....

....

....

Am I tempted to judge this feeling? Can I pause and just be with it? How does that feel?

....

....

....

....

Does this feeling cause an urge to perform any actions or behaviors? If so, what are they? Can I explain why? Are these positive responses?

....

....

....

....

....

How long did this feeling last?

....

When this feeling started

|

When it ended

Did this feeling appear and disappear gradually or abruptly?

....

Do I expect to feel this way again?

....

Any other notes I want to add about this feeling:

....

....

....

....

....

....

Date: .... *Time:* ....

Right now I am feeling (list all the feelings and sensations that apply):

....

....

....

....

....

....

....

A word from the Feelings List on page 12 or a short sentence that best describes the state I'm in or what I am experiencing:

....

....

Intensity of this feeling:

low-key					real				fierce

How my body feels:

....

....

....

....

....

Are there any visual images I associate with this feeling? If so, draw or color below:

Is there a song or a piece of music that reflects this feeling?

....

Would I describe the feeling as positive, neutral, or negative? Why?

....

....

....

What do I think caused or influenced this feeling?

....

....

....

....

Does this feeling bring up anything from my past?

....

....

....

....

Is this feeling uncomfortable in any way? If so, how?

....

....

....

....

Am I tempted to judge this feeling? Can I pause and just be with it? How does that feel?

....

....

....

....

Does this feeling cause an urge to perform any actions or behaviors? If so, what are they? Can I explain why? Are these positive responses?

....

....

....

....

....

How long did this feeling last?

....

When this feeling started

|

When it ended

Did this feeling appear and disappear gradually or abruptly?

....

Do I expect to feel this way again?

....

Any other notes I want to add about this feeling:

....
....
....
....
....
....

Date:.. Time:.................................

Right now I am feeling (list all the feelings and sensations that apply):

....

....

....

....

....

....

....

A word from the Feelings List on page 12 or a short sentence that best describes
the state I'm in or what I am experiencing:

....

....

Intensity of this feeling:

low-key   real   fierce

How my body feels:

....

....

....

....

....

Are there any visual images I associate with this feeling? If so, draw or color below:

Is there a song or a piece of music that reflects this feeling?

....

Would I describe the feeling as positive, neutral, or negative? Why?

....

....

....

What do I think caused or influenced this feeling?

....

....

....

....

Does this feeling bring up anything from my past?

....

....

....

....

Is this feeling uncomfortable in any way? If so, how?

....

....

....

....

Am I tempted to judge this feeling? Can I pause and just be with it? How does that feel?

....

....

....

....

Does this feeling cause an urge to perform any actions or behaviors? If so, what are they? Can I explain why? Are these positive responses?

....

....

....

....

....

How long did this feeling last?

....

When this feeling started

|

|

When it ended

Did this feeling appear and disappear gradually or abruptly?

....

Do I expect to feel this way again?

....

Any other notes I want to add about this feeling:

....

....

....

....

....

....

Date: .... Time: ....

Right now I am feeling (list all the feelings and sensations that apply):

....

....

....

....

....

....

....

A word from the Feelings List on page 12 or a short sentence that best describes the state I'm in or what I am experiencing:

....

....

Intensity of this feeling:

low-key   real   fierce

How my body feels:

....

....

....

....

....

Are there any visual images I associate with this feeling? If so, draw or color below:

Is there a song or a piece of music that reflects this feeling?

....

Would I describe the feeling as positive, neutral, or negative? Why?

....

....

....

What do I think caused or influenced this feeling?

....

....

....

....

Does this feeling bring up anything from my past?

....

....

....

....

Is this feeling uncomfortable in any way? If so, how?

....

....

....

....

Am I tempted to judge this feeling? Can I pause and just be with it? How does that feel?

....

....

....

....

Does this feeling cause an urge to perform any actions or behaviors? If so, what are they? Can I explain why? Are these positive responses?

....

....

....

....

....

How long did this feeling last?

....

When this feeling started

When it ended

Did this feeling appear and disappear gradually or abruptly?

....

Do I expect to feel this way again?

....

Any other notes I want to add about this feeling:

....

....

....

....

....

....

Date:... Time:..................................

Right now I am feeling (list all the feelings and sensations that apply):

....

....

....

....

....

....

....

A word from the Feelings List on page 12 or a short sentence that best describes
the state I'm in or what I am experiencing:

....

....

Intensity of this feeling:

low-key   real   fierce

How my body feels:

....

....

....

....

....

Are there any visual images I associate with this feeling? If so, draw or color below:

Is there a song or a piece of music that reflects this feeling?

....

Would I describe the feeling as positive, neutral, or negative? Why?

....

....

....

What do I think caused or influenced this feeling?

....

....

....

....

Does this feeling bring up anything from my past?

....

....

....

....

Is this feeling uncomfortable in any way? If so, how?

....

....

....

....

Am I tempted to judge this feeling? Can I pause and just be with it? How does that feel?

....

....

....

....

Does this feeling cause an urge to perform any actions or behaviors? If so, what are they? Can I explain why? Are these positive responses?

....

....

....

....

....

How long did this feeling last?

....

When this feeling started

|

When it ended

Did this feeling appear and disappear gradually or abruptly?

....

Do I expect to feel this way again?

....

Any other notes I want to add about this feeling:

....

....

....

....

....

....

Date: .... *Time:* ....

Right now I am feeling (list all the feelings and sensations that apply):

....

....

....

....

....

....

....

A word from the Feelings List on page 12 or a short sentence that best describes the state I'm in or what I am experiencing:

....

....

Intensity of this feeling:

low-key   real   fierce

How my body feels:

....

....

....

....

....

Are there any visual images I associate with this feeling? If so, draw or color below:

Is there a song or a piece of music that reflects this feeling?

....

Would I describe the feeling as positive, neutral, or negative? Why?

....

....

....

What do I think caused or influenced this feeling?

....

....

....

....

Does this feeling bring up anything from my past?

....

....

....

....

Is this feeling uncomfortable in any way? If so, how?

....

....

....

....

Am I tempted to judge this feeling? Can I pause and just be with it? How does that feel?

....

....

....

....

Does this feeling cause an urge to perform any actions or behaviors? If so, what are they? Can I explain why? Are these positive responses?

....

....

....

....

....

How long did this feeling last?

....

When this feeling started

When it ended

Did this feeling appear and disappear gradually or abruptly?

....

Do I expect to feel this way again?

....

Any other notes I want to add about this feeling:

....

....

....

....

....

....

Date:.. Time:.................................

Right now I am feeling (list all the feelings and sensations that apply):

....

....

....

....

....

....

....

A word from the Feelings List on page 12 or a short sentence that best describes the state I'm in or what I am experiencing:

....

....

Intensity of this feeling:

low-key   real   fierce

How my body feels:

....

....

....

....

....

Are there any visual images I associate with this feeling? If so, draw or color below:

Is there a song or a piece of music that reflects this feeling?

....

Would I describe the feeling as positive, neutral, or negative? Why?

....

....

....

What do I think caused or influenced this feeling?

....

....

....

....

Does this feeling bring up anything from my past?

....

....

....

....

Is this feeling uncomfortable in any way? If so, how?

....

....

....

....

Am I tempted to judge this feeling? Can I pause and just be with it? How does that feel?

....

....

....

....

Does this feeling cause an urge to perform any actions or behaviors? If so, what are they? Can I explain why? Are these positive responses?

....

....

....

....

....

How long did this feeling last?

....

When this feeling started

|

When it ended

Did this feeling appear and disappear gradually or abruptly?

....

Do I expect to feel this way again?

....

Any other notes I want to add about this feeling:

....

....

....

....

....

....

Date: .... *Time:* ....

Right now I am feeling (list all the feelings and sensations that apply):

....

....

....

....

....

....

....

A word from the Feelings List on page 12 or a short sentence that best describes the state I'm in or what I am experiencing:

....

....

Intensity of this feeling:

low-key .... real .... fierce

How my body feels:

....

....

....

....

....

Are there any visual images I associate with this feeling? If so, draw or color below:

Is there a song or a piece of music that reflects this feeling?

....

Would I describe the feeling as positive, neutral, or negative? Why?

....

....

....

What do I think caused or influenced this feeling?

....

....

....

....

Does this feeling bring up anything from my past?

....
....
....
....

Is this feeling uncomfortable in any way? If so, how?

....
....
....
....

Am I tempted to judge this feeling? Can I pause and just be with it? How does that feel?

....
....
....
....

Does this feeling cause an urge to perform any actions or behaviors? If so, what are they? Can I explain why? Are these positive responses?

....
....
....
....
....

How long did this feeling last?

....

When this feeling started

When it ended

Did this feeling appear and disappear gradually or abruptly?

....

Do I expect to feel this way again?

....

Any other notes I want to add about this feeling:

....

....

....

....

....

....

Date: .... Time: ....

Right now I am feeling (list all the feelings and sensations that apply):

....

....

....

....

....

....

....

A word from the Feelings List on page 12 or a short sentence that best describes the state I'm in or what I am experiencing:

....

....

Intensity of this feeling:

low-key   real   fierce

How my body feels:

....

....

....

....

....

Are there any visual images I associate with this feeling? If so, draw or color below:

Is there a song or a piece of music that reflects this feeling?

....

Would I describe the feeling as positive, neutral, or negative? Why?

....

....

....

What do I think caused or influenced this feeling?

....

....

....

....

Does this feeling bring up anything from my past?

....

....

....

....

Is this feeling uncomfortable in any way? If so, how?

....

....

....

....

Am I tempted to judge this feeling? Can I pause and just be with it? How does that feel?

....

....

....

....

Does this feeling cause an urge to perform any actions or behaviors? If so, what are they? Can I explain why? Are these positive responses?

....

....

....

....

....

How long did this feeling last?

....

When this feeling started

|

When it ended

Did this feeling appear and disappear gradually or abruptly?

....

Do I expect to feel this way again?

....

Any other notes I want to add about this feeling:

....

....

....

....

....

....

Date: .... Time: ....

Right now I am feeling (list all the feelings and sensations that apply):

....

....

....

....

....

....

....

A word from the Feelings List on page 12 or a short sentence that best describes the state I'm in or what I am experiencing:

....

....

Intensity of this feeling:

low-key				real				fierce

How my body feels:

....

....

....

....

....

Are there any visual images I associate with this feeling? If so, draw or color below:

Is there a song or a piece of music that reflects this feeling?

....

Would I describe the feeling as positive, neutral, or negative? Why?

....

....

....

What do I think caused or influenced this feeling?

....

....

....

....

Does this feeling bring up anything from my past?

....
....
....
....

Is this feeling uncomfortable in any way? If so, how?

....
....
....
....

Am I tempted to judge this feeling? Can I pause and just be with it? How does that feel?

....
....
....
....

Does this feeling cause an urge to perform any actions or behaviors? If so, what are they? Can I explain why? Are these positive responses?

....
....
....
....
....

How long did this feeling last?

....

When this feeling started

|

When it ended

Did this feeling appear and disappear gradually or abruptly?

....

Do I expect to feel this way again?

....

Any other notes I want to add about this feeling:

....

....

....

....

....

....

Date:.. Time:.................................

Right now I am feeling (list all the feelings and sensations that apply):

....

....

....

....

....

....

....

A word from the Feelings List on page 12 or a short sentence that best describes the state I'm in or what I am experiencing:

....

....

Intensity of this feeling:

low-key ———————————— real ———————————— fierce

How my body feels:

....

....

....

....

....

Are there any visual images I associate with this feeling? If so, draw or color below:

Is there a song or a piece of music that reflects this feeling?

....

Would I describe the feeling as positive, neutral, or negative? Why?

....

....

....

What do I think caused or influenced this feeling?

....

....

....

....

Does this feeling bring up anything from my past?

....
....
....
....

Is this feeling uncomfortable in any way? If so, how?

....
....
....
....

Am I tempted to judge this feeling? Can I pause and just be with it? How does that feel?

....
....
....
....

Does this feeling cause an urge to perform any actions or behaviors? If so, what are they? Can I explain why? Are these positive responses?

....
....
....
....
....

How long did this feeling last?

....

When this feeling started

|

When it ended

Did this feeling appear and disappear gradually or abruptly?

....

Do I expect to feel this way again?

....

Any other notes I want to add about this feeling:

....

....

....

....

....

....

Mental Health Resources

Crisis support lines

United States
988 Suicide and Crisis Lifeline
Call, text, or chat 988 for the Lifeline, which provides 24/7, free, and confidential support for people in crisis or experiencing emotional distress.

Mental Health Support
Call 24/7 for trained counselors who will listen, provide support, and connect callers to resources.
For English, call: 1-800-273-TALK (8255)
En Español, call: 1-888-628-9454
For deaf or hard of hearing, call:
1-800-799-4889

Canada
The Canada Suicide Prevention Service
Call: 1-833-456-4566
Text: 45645
Phone line available 24 hours. Texting available 4 p.m. to midnight ET.

Worldwide
Suicide Hotlines and Prevention Resources Around the World
www.psychologytoday.com/us /basics/suicide/suicide-prevention -hotlines-resources-worldwide

Nonurgent resources for finding mental health care

National Institute of Mental Health: www.nimh.nih.gov

Canadian Mental Health Association: https://cmha.ca

Find a Therapist: www.psychologytoday.com/us/therapists

Further Reading

Abblett, Mitch, PhD. "Tame Reactive Emotions by Naming Them," *Mindful.org*, September 25, 2019, www.mindful.org /labels-help-tame-reactive-emotions-naming.

Ackerman, Courtney E., MA. "83 Benefits of Journaling for Depression, Anxiety, and Stress," *PositivePsychology.com*, May 14, 2018, www.positivepsychology.com/benefits-of-journaling.

Damasio, Antonio R., MD, PhD. "The Science of Emotion,"
LC/NIMH Decade of the Brain Project, May 5, 1998,
www.loc.gov/loc/brain/emotion/Damasio.html.

Doucleff, Michaeleen. "Stuck in a Rut? Sometimes Joy Takes
a Little Practice," *Morning Edition*, June 29, 2021,
www.npr.org/sections/health-shots/2021/06/29/1010319240
/stuck-in-a-rut-sometimes-joy-takes-a-little-practice.

Firestone, Lisa, PhD. "Name It to Tame It: The Emotions Underlying
Your Triggers," *PyschologyToday.com*, February 1, 2022,
www.psychologytoday.com/us/blog/compassion-matters/202202
/name-it-tame-it-the-emotions-underlying-your-triggers.

Lieberman, Matthew D., Naomi I. Eisenberger, Molly J. Crockett,
Sabrina M. Tom, Jennifer H. Pfeifer, and Baldwin M. Way. "Putting Feelings
into Words: Affect Labeling Disrupts Amygdala Activity in Response to
Affective Stimuli," *Psychological Science*, June 30, 2006,
www.scn.ucla.edu/pdf/AL(2007).pdf.

Lieberman, Matthew D., Tristen K. Inagaki, Golnaz Tabibnia, and
Molly J. Crockett. "Subjective Responses to Emotional Stimuli
During Labeling, Reappraisal, and Distraction," *Emotion*, June 2011,
doi.apa.org/fulltext/2011-08959-001.html.

Pressman, Peter, MD. "The Science of Emotions: How the Brain
Shapes How You Feel," *Verywell Health*, February 27, 2022,
www.verywellhealth.com/the-science-of-emotions-2488708.

Schwartz, Tony. "The Importance of Naming Your Emotions,"
New York Times, April 3, 2015, www.nytimes.com/2015/04/04
/business/dealbook/the-importance-of-naming-your-emotions.html.

University of California, Los Angeles. "Putting Feelings into Words
Produces Therapeutic Effects in the Brain." *ScienceDaily*, June 22, 2007,
www.sciencedaily.com/releases/2007/06/070622090727.htm.

Printed in China

SPRUCE BOOKS with colophon is a registered trademark of
Penguin Random House LLC

27 26 25 24 23 22   9 8 7 6 5 4 3 2 1

Editor: Sharyn Rosart
Production editor: Rachelle Longé McGhee
Designer: Alison Keefe
Illustrations: © Tina Bits / Adobe Stock

ISBN: 978-1-63217-469-7

Spruce Books, a Sasquatch Books Imprint
1325 Fourth Avenue, Suite 1025, Seattle, WA 98101

SasquatchBooks.com

MIX
Paper | Supporting
responsible forestry
FSC® C008047
FSC
www.fsc.org